The Tragedy of

or

The Life and Death of the Great Tom Thumb

a burlesque

by

Henry Fielding

as re-told

by

Dedwydd Jones

1707 – 1754

by HOGARTH 1762

FOREWORD

by

Henry Fielding

This city has seldom been so divided in its opinion concerning the merit of the following acts and scenes of my piece *The Great Sir Tom Thumb*. While some publically affirmed that no author could have produced so fine a piece as Mr Henry Fielding; others have vehemently insisted that no one could have written anything as bad as Mr Fielding. Nor can we wonder about this dissension about its merit while the learned world has not even decided on the nature of Tragedy itself. For though most of the universities in Europe have honoured it, praising it as the highest and most outstanding work and the famous Professor Burman has styled *Sir Tom Thumb* as 'possessing the most heroic qualities of Tragedy.' Among other languages, it has been translated into Dutch and celebrated with great applause at Amsterdam – where burlesque itself had never actually reached. Under the title of *Mynheer Vander Thumb*, the worthy burgomasters received it with that reverent and silent attention which so becomes all audiences of tragedy. Yet notwithstanding all this, there have not beenwanting some who have represented these marvellous Tom Thumb's scenes in a ludicrous light. The Poet Laureate himself was heard to say , with some concern, that he wondered that such a tragical and Christian nation as ours would permit the representation on its stages a version so visibly designed to ridicule and extirpate everything that is great and solemn among us. And why? This learned critic and his followers were led into so great an error by that surreptitious and piratical copy which stole into the world last year, with such injustice and prejudice to our author. I hope this will be acknowledges by everyone who shall now happily peruse the genuine and original copy presented here. Nor can I help remarking to the great praise of our author, that however imperfect the former copy was, it still reflected the resemblance of the true *Tom Thumb* and contained sufficient beauties to give it a run of two hundred and forty performances to the politest of audiences. But in spite of the applause which it received from the best judges, it was severely censured by some few bad ones, and I believe rather maliciously than ignorantly, and reported to have been intended as a 'burlesque' on the loftiest parts of tragedy and designed to banish what we generally call 'fine things' from our stage. Now, if I can set my country right in an affair of this importance, I shall lightly esteem any labour which it may cost. And I undertake this, firstly, as it is indeed in some measure incumbent on me to vindicate myself from that afore mentioned surreptitious copy, published by some ill-meaning people under my name! Secondly, knowing myself more capable of doing justice to our author than any other man, as I have given myself more pains to arrive at a thorough understanding of this little piece, Tom Thumb, having for ten years read nothing else! - in which time I think I may modestly presume, with the help of my English dictionary, to comprehend all the meanings of every word in it.

But should any error of my pen awaken any critic to enlighten the world with his annotations on our author, I shall not consider it the least reward or happiness arising to me from these, my endeavours. I shall avoid at present those things which have caused such feuds in the world of learning – whether this play was originally written by Shakespeare – which certainly, if it were true, would certainly add a considerable share to its merit, especially with such who are so generous as to buy and to commend what they never read, from an implicit faith in the Author only – a faith which our age abounds in, as much as it can be called 'deficient' in any other. Let it suffice that the Tragedy of Tragedies or The Life and Death of Tom Thumb was written in the reign of Queen Elizabeth I. Nor can the objection made by the academic Mr Wright, that the tragedy must then have been antecedent to the official history, have any weight, when we consider, that tho' the history of Tom Thumb, printed by and for Edward Meek at the *Looking Glass* on London Bridge, be of a later date, we must still suppose this version to have been transcribed from some other source, unless we suppose the writer thereof to be inspired the beauty of the matter. But this is a gift very faintly contended by the writers of our age. As to this history not bearing the stamp of second, third or fourth edition, I see but little in this objection, for editions are very uncertain lights to judge books by. Perhaps Mr Meek may have joined twenty editions into one, as Mr Wright has now divided one into twenty. Nor does the other argument, drawn from the little care our author has taken to keep to the letter of his history, carry any greater force. Aren't there instances of plays wherein the histories are so perverted that we can know the heroes whom they celebrate by no other marks than their names? No, we do not find the same character placed by different poets in such different lights that we can discover not the least sameness, or even likeness in the features? The *Sophonisba* of Mairet and of Lee, is a tender, amorous, passionate mistress of Massinissa; Corneille and Mr Thomson give her no other passion but love of her country and make her as cool in her affection to Massinissa, as to Syphax. In the two latter, she resembles the character of Queen Elizabeth; in the two former she is the picture of Mary Queen of Scots. In short, the one Sophinisba is as different from the other as the Brutus of Voltaire is from the Marius Junior of Otway, or as the Minerva is from the Venus of the ancients – just a little aside for academic clarity's sake. Let us now proceed to a regular examination of the tragedy before us. I shall treat separately of the fable or plot, the moral, the characters, the sentiments and of the diction. First, the fable or plot- which I take to be the most simple imaginable. To use the words of an eminent author, 'one regular and uniform fable, not charged with a multiplicity of incidents and yet affording several revolutions of fortune by which the passions may be excited, varied and driven to the full tumult of emotion.' Nor is the action of this tragedy less great than uniform. The spring of all is the love of Tom Thumb for Princess Honeycombe Awena, which caused the quarrel between their Majesties in the first Act, the passion of Colonel Farr-Parr Grizzle, in the second; the rebellion and fall of Colonel Grizzle and the giantess Corporanda, and that bloody catastrophe in the third, the bloody devouring of Tom Thumb. Nor is the moral of this excellent tragedy less noble than the plot. It teaches two instructive lessons, ie, that human happiness is extremely transient and that death is the certain end of all men - the former fate illustrated by the fatal end of Tom Thumb and the latter, by that of all other personages on stage. The characters are I think sufficiently described in the Dramatis Personae. You will find few plays where greater care is taken to maintain that punctiliousness throughout and to preserve in every speech that characteristical mark which distinguishes them from each other. And says our wise critic, Mr C, 'how well does the character of Tom Thumb, whom we must call the hero of this tragedy, if there is one, agrees with Aristotle's Precepts, in which tragedy is defined as being 'the imitation of a short but perfect action, containing a just greatness in itself.' What greatness then can be in a fellow, which History tells us is no higher than an ape. This gentleman seems to think that the greatness of a man's soul is in proportion to his body, but this I assure you is disputed by our English physognominical writers. Besides, if I understand Aristotle right, he is speaking only of greatness of action and not of the person. As for the sentiments and the diction, which now only remain to be mentioned, I thought I could afford them no stronger justification than by producing parallel passages out of the best of our English writers. Whether this sameness of thought and expression which I have quoted from them, proceeded from an agreement to their way of thinking, or whether I have borrowed from our author, I leave the observer to determine. I shall venture to affirm this of the sentiments of our author – that they are generally the most familiar which I have ever met with, and at the same time delivered with the highest dignity of phrase! - this leads me on to speak of his diction and here I shall make but one postulate –

that the greatest perfection of the language of a tragedy is that it is not understood, which granted, as I think it must be, it will necessarily follow that the only ways to avoid this is by being too high or too low for the understanding, which will include every thing within its reach. These two extremities of style, the Poet Laureate illustrates with his familar image of two Inns, which I shall term the 'Aerial' and the 'Subterrestrial.' Horace goes farther and shows when it is proper to call in at one of these Inns and when at the other. He clearly approves of what he calls the 'Sesquipedalia' style because some authirs used this diction in prosperity and could hardly have dropped it in adversity. The 'Aerial' Inn therefore is only to be visited by Princes and other great men of the highest affluence of fortune; the 'subterrestrial' is appointed for the entertainment of th poorer sort of people, the proles, as in Roman times, Horace again observes. The true meanings of these Horatian quotes is that bombast is the proper language for Joy, and doggerel for grief. Cicero highly recommends this Aerial diction, for he asks what can be so proper for Tragedy as a set of big-sounding words so mixed up together as to convey no meaning at all - which as Ovid himself agrees, declaring he would show one day the divine presence in the 'Aerial.' Moreover, Tragedy of all writings has the greatest share in Bathos, so say the scribblers, but I shall not presume to determine which of these two styles be right for Tragedy , suffice it to say that our author excels in both. He very rarely intrudes himself throughout the whole play, either rising higher than the eye of your understanding can soar, or sinking lower than it can stoop. But here it might be said, that I have given more frequent instances of Authors who have imitated our author in the sublime, than in the opposite - to which I answer something like this - first, bombast being properly a redundancy of genius, instances of nature occur in poets whose names do more honour to our author than the writers in doggerel, for his chosen style proceeds from a cool, calm, weighty way of thinking. The opposite of this are most frequently noted in Authors of the lower class, the untutored proles - if the works of such low types can be found at all. Furthermore, it is a very hard task to read them in order to attempt to extract some blossoms of beauty from them, and finally, it is very difficult to transplant them, because like some flowers, they are so delicate in nature they can flourish in no soil but their own. For it is easy enough to transcribe a thought but not the want of one. The good Earl of Essex, for example, has a little garden of choice rarities, from which you can barely transplant one line so as to preserve its original beauty. This must account to the Reader for his missing the names of several of his literary acquaintances which he would certainly found here if I had read their works. However, the reader may meet with due satisfaction on this point for I have a young undergraduate and commentator, who is currently reading over all the modern tragedies, at five shillings a dozen, and recovering all they have stolen from our author, which we shall shortly be adding as an Appendix to this Preface.

(*ENTER SPY*, in 18th century costume, with cane and surveys the scene with hostility. The 'SPY' in fact is SIR ROBERT WALPOLE, PRIME MINISTER, unrecognised by AUDIENCE until the final curtain!)

SPY: Now let us leap straight into the Dramatis Personae! *(Reads out cast list)* The men first: ARTHUR II, KING of the Brythons, a passionate sort of man, husband of QUEEN DOLLALLOLLA; ARTHUR II stands a little in fear of his QUEEN; KING and QUEEN are parents of PRINCESS HONEYCOMBE HUNCAMUNCA , of whom KING ARTHUR is very fond; ARTHUR II is in love with GLUMDALCA, captive QUEEN OF A TRIBE Of GIANTS, a giantess herself; 'the name of the game' GENERAL TOM THUMB THE GREAT, a little hero with a great soul, a bit violent in his temper, which is soothed somewhat by his love for his adored PRINCESS HONEYCOMBE HUNCAMNCA; GHOST of KING ARTHUR's ancestors, a whimsical kind of family apparition; GHOST is also TOM THUMB's magical mentor, the Taff wizard MERLIN; the two-faced, rebel leader, COLONEL FARR-PARR GRIZZLE, extremely zealous for the liberty of the subject, especially if under his control, very bad-tempered and in love with PRINCESS HONEYCOMBE; GRIZZLE is a traitor to the end; COURTIERS and PLACEMEN, NOODLE and DOODLE; DOODLE in love with MUSTACHA, CHIEF LADY-IN -WAVING; Ist and 2nd PHYSICIANS, DOCTORS FILLGRAVE and GRAVEYARD; 1st, 2nd BAILIFFS; the SPY, SIR ROBERT WALPOLE; various COURTIERS, PETITIONERS, SOLDIERS, SERVANTS.

And now to the Ladies:

QUEEN DOLLALLOLLA , wife of KING ARTHUR II, mother of PRINCESS HONEYCOMBE HUNCAMUNCA; QUEEN DOLLALLOLLA is an entirely faultless woman except she is a bit given to drink and is a little too much of a virago towards her husband; she is also in love with GENERAL TOM THUMB the GREAT; the PRINCESS HONEYCOMBE HUNCAMUNCA, who is of a very generous, and amorous disposition, equally in love with TOM THUMB and COLONEL FARR-PARR GRIZZLE, rebel pretender; the PRINCESS desperately wants to marry both; GLUMDALCA , OF A NEARBY TRIBE of giants, now captive, QUEEN GLUMDALCA beloved of the KING, but GLUMDALCA is also in love with the mighty TOM THUMB; MUSTACHA, MAID OF HONOUR, CHIEF LADY-IN-WAVING, in love with DOODLE, waves royally in every scene.

To the Plot, Fable or Action now! Enjoy!

(EXIT SPY)

ACT 1 SCENE 1

(Court of KING ARTHUR II, throne room of the Palace of Buckingham, set on a spreading green plain. Sound of trumpets, drums, cheering off stage; ENTER fawning COURTIERS, DOODLE and NOODLE. They look in the direction of the cheering)

DOODLE: I tell you, such a time as this was never seen!

NOODLE: The sun himself on this divine appointed day, Shines on a real General in his new armoured suit, Dressed to the nines, decorated for the masses, Praised to the skies, the silly bloody asses...

DOODLE: ...so Nature wears one universal grin for him!

DOODLE, NOODLE: Hip, Hip Hooray! This day, Master Doodle, is a day indeed...

DOODLE: ...a day we never saw before ...

NOODLE: ...a day of royal pageantry and awe!

DOODLE: ...look! The mighty Thomas Thumb victorious comes, See, millions of giants crowd beneath his chariot wheels.

The true Gigantics! to whom the giants of Whitehall are infant dwarfs!

As when some cock-sparrow in a farmer's yard Hops at the head of this huge flock of turkeys, Which frown and foam and roar like the pretender Grizzle While Tom regardless of their noise rides on.

DOODLE: When good Father Thumb first brought this Thomas forth, The genius of our land triumphant reigned;

O, yes, our Arthur II, was all for me and you!

NOODLE: They tell me it is whispered in the books Of all our advisers, that this mighty hero By Taff Merlin's spells begot, Does not have a single bone beneath his skin, Just a bunch of useless gristle stuck within.

DOODLE: Then it is gristle of no mortal kind, Some god, my Noodle, stepped into the place Of gaffer Thumb who only half-begot This mighty Tom.

NOODLE: I am convinced he was sent express from heaven To be a pillar of our state, by divine right, alright.

Although Tom's body is so very small The leg of a chair is more than twice as large as his, Yet is his soul like any mountain – big, And as a mountain once brought forth a mouse, So does this mouse a mighty mountain now contains.

DOODLE: Mountain indeed! So terrible is Tom's name, Gentle nurses and nannies frighten babies with it And cry 'you naughty one, Tom Thumb is come And if you re naughty once again, You'll go to bed in dire and bloody pain!'

NOODLE: Listen to those marvellous bugles, Fanfares of the King's approaches.

DOODLE: He's in time for my petition, The Chamberlain's job is my position.

NOODLE: No, it's mine.

DOODLE: Mine I say...look at it from all sides then, Doodle, Palaces and mansions, like stables and sties Can still be the haunt of asses and flies.

And don' forget, MP's and Premiers, too, All have their price, like me, like you, banked in a trice!

NOODLE: With you there, bro. Gimme five!

DOODLE: The Marshall of the Fleshpots now arrives, Job Dispenser number one, Be kindly to his Highness as to no other.

ACT I SCENE 2

(ENTER KING ARTHUR II, QUEEN DOLLALLOLLA, in fab ermine and crowns, COLONEL FARR-PARR GRIZZLE, and COURTIERS. All drunk, slur words, hiccup, some with glasses, gulp booze, wave bottles, fawn and bow to the royals as they sit on the throne. MUSTACHA, CHIEF LADY- -IN-WAVING waves to audience, royally throughout)

KING ARTHUR: *(on throne)* Let nothing but a face of joy appear today, The man who frowns in this happy hour Will lose his head, not to say his tongue, So he'll have no face with which to frown at all And no speech to grace the honour of Tom Thumb.

Smile Dollallolla, dear! Hey, what wrinkled sorrow hangs, Sits, lies, frowns upon your knitted brows?

And why these tears all down your blubbery cheek Like swollen gutters gushing in the streets?

QUEEN DOLLALLOLLA: I've heard folks say, my Lord, That excess of joy makes tears As much as excess of grief.

KING ARTHUR: If that is so, let all men cry for joy, Until my whole court is drowned in tears!

Yes, until they overflow my farthest lands And leave me nothing but the sea to rule!

DOODLE: I have here an eloquent petition, Sire.

KING ARTHUR: You don't say!

DOODLE: Have I got the Chamberlain's boss's job at last?

KING ARTHUR: Petition me no petitions today, sir, Let other hours be set aside for business. Today it is our pleasure to be drunk And here our Queen shall be as pissed as we.

DOLLALLOLLA: *(Aside)* I'm half three sheets to the wind already.

But if the next capacious goblet overflows With punch, by George, I'll swig it down!

Rum and brandy I won't touch a drop, Why Punch is two shillings a quart, And rum and brandy up to six, New gin leaves you half dead, one tot Is the cheapest and the deadliest of the lot...

KING ARTHUR: *(Aside)* ... how the cringing hypocrites fawn on me.

The sunshine of a court can in a day, Ripen the vilest insect to an eagle, And every little wretch who but an hour Ago had scorned and trod me under foot, Shall lift his eyes aloft and gazing at the throne, Flatter what they scorned a short hour before.

FARR-PARR GRIZZLE: *(aside)* I don't mind bowing to the ground And welcome treason when it's sound, My Regiments are still my bestest friends, True sons of Liberty! - swords and daggers all, The lair is laid, I'm off, with them, to final victory!

(EXIT FARR-PARR GRIZZLE. DOODLE EXITS after FARR-PARR, has a word with him and immediately RE-ENTERS, nodding thoughtfully)

DOODLE: I've had a further order from clever Grizzle, there, He'd already set up bailiffs, two or more, Who'll leave Tom Thumb both bruised and sore;

Just as Dollallolla wishes, tho' she keeps silent as a nun, She also dotes on various aspects of the Great Tom Thumb, But just to teach the lesson - royalty is always served!

But I did not like having my petition cast aside, LIke an empty lobster's claw at a forbidden feast, either.

NOODLE: Neither did I.

DOODLE: I'm off, like the man called Farr-Parr, with huge preferment on my mind.

NOODLE: Ditto and likewise.

KING ARTHUR: Doodle and Noodle, honey locusts both, Like two snakes in the grass you are, Worse than bloody gnats, so bugger off!

(EXIT DOODLE, NOODLE fawning. MUSTASHA waves)

KING ARTHUR: ...but rather than quarrel about the price of pots, My Queen, you will have your way, Roll out the barrel! *(ALL cheer)* But look who's coming now, The great Tom Thumb at last!

You mini-hero, you giant-killing boy, The saviour of my Kingdom, has arrived!

(ALL cheer, toast)

ACT 1 SCENE III

(ENTER TOM THUMB flourishing a bottle and a battle-axe, with OFFICERS; GLUMDALCA captive GIANT QUEEN, in chains)

KING ARTHUR: O, welcome, Tom, welcome to my arms!

> What rewards of gratitude can thank away All the debt your valour lays on me.

DOLLALLOLLA *(aside, of TOM)*: O God, he's gorgeous.

TOM THUMB: When I am not thanked at all, I am thanked enough, I've done my duty and I've done no more.

DOLLALLOLLA: *(Aside)* I've never heard such a godlike idol speak!

KING ARTHUR: Your modesty is like a candle, boy, It illuminates itself and shows your virtues too.

> But tell me, boy, where did you leave the giants?

TOM THUMB: Outside the arches of the castle gates, my Liege, Which are too low for them to pass through.

KING ARTHUR: What do these foreigners look like?

TOM THUMB: Like nothing but themselves.

DOLLOLALLA: *(Aside)* And you certainly are nothing like anybody else, lovely boy!

KING ARTHUR: Enough of this chatter! *(Aside)* A vast vision now fills my soul, I see them, yes, the giants, now before me, The monstrous, ugly, barbarous, sons of whores!

(GLUMDALCA comes forward)

> But what's this majestic form that rises up before our eyes?

> So perfect it seems the gods on Mount Olympus were present At her birth; and when delivered all cried out "This is a woman!"

(GLUMDALCA's chains fall off. ALL cheer)

TOM THUMB: Then the gods were mistaken - she is not a woman But a giantess, Glumdalca by name, who we strained to drag inside the town, For she is a foot taller than all her subject hairy mammoths.

GLUMDALCA: Alas, yesterday we were both Queen and wife, With one hundred thousand giants at our finger tips, Twenty of which I was happily married to ourself.

DOLLALLOLLA: What a happy state of giantism – where husbands Like mushroom grow, while, awful fate, we are forced to take But one - unless it be the lovely boy, Tom Thumb, for me.

GLUMDALCA: But to lose them all in one black day!

The sun that rose saw me wife to twenty giants, And when setting saw me widowed of them all, My heart is worn-out and like a leaking ship One more drop of water, we will quickly sink.

DOLLALLOLLA: Madame, believe me,

I look upon your sorrows with a woman's eye.

But now learn to act with all the strength you have, For tomorrow we will have all our Grenadiers drawn up in line, And choose as many husbands as you like, absolutely fine, believe me.

GLUMDALCA: Madame, it will be done! I am still your most humble and obedient servant!

DOLLALLOLLA: Wave, Mustacha, wave, you are not Chief Lady-in-Waving for nothing!

KING ARTHUR: My alien and curvaceous Queen Glumdalca, Go now, but regard this court as your own, Do not do not look on me as a tyrant Landlord of a royal Inn, Order freely any drink, there'll be nothing to pay – go now

(EXIT QUEEN GLUMDALCA)

KING ARTHUR: Jesus Christ, I feel a sudden pain inside my chest, Ah! I do not know whether it comes from love, Or if it's just a burping-fit - time alone will tell.

O Thumb, now tell us, what do we owe to your valour, Ask for such a huge reward, no monarch can deny!

TOM THUMB: I don't want Kingdoms, I can conquer those, I don't want money, I've got plenty of that, But for what I've done, and what I mean to do, For giants killed, and giants yet unborn, Which I will slaughter, and If this is Debt, Reward my request in full – I ask but this – To sun myself in Huncamunca's limpid eyes!

KING ARTHUR: What a prodigious bold request!

DOLLALLOLLA: *(Aside)* Be still, my beating breast!

TOM THUMB: My heart is at the threshold of your mouth And waits for its answer there. O, don't frown, I've tried to tune my breast with reason, but broke the strings, But I say to you, even if Jove himself had shouted out, 'you shan't have her,' I would have loved her all the more!

What a strange fate, that when I loved her least, I loved her most, another bloody paradox!

KING ARTHUR: It is decided – the Princess is your own!

TOM THUMB: Oh, happy, happy, happy, happy Thumb!!

DOLLALLOLLA: But my Leige, consider - reward your Grenadiers, Yes, but do not give sweet Huncamunca to Tom Thumb!

KING ARTHUR: 'Tom Thumb!' my wide and ever growing realm, Does not know a name so glorious as 'Tom Thumb!' Macedonia had Alexander, Rome her Caesar, France her sun-king, Holland her Mynheers, Ireland her 'O's', Scotland her 'Mac's,' Wales her

Taffs, But let England boast no other name but 'Tom Thumb!'

DOLLALLOLLA: *(ASIDE)* However swollen with virtue his character is, He shall not have my darling daughter!

KING ARTHUR: You talkin' about our dear Huncamunca?

DOLLALOLLA: I say you shall not have her, that's for sure.

KING ARTHUR: Then by our royal self, we swear you lie.

DOLLALLOLLA: Who but a dog would treat me as you do, Me, who laid so randy by your side these twenty years or so.

But I will be revenged, I will see you hanged!

So now tremble all of you who were for this match, For like a cat in the topmost boughs, I'll squat and squirt down royal vengeance on you all, Piss on the lot of you!

(EXIT in fury)

KING ARTHUR: *(Aside)* My god, the Queen is in a passion, And without benefit of toilet. But whether she is or not, I'll see my daughter now, and pave the way for Thumb.

Yes, I'd look a pretty ripe wimp to give in to her will, When by force or art, the wife overreach the man, Then let him wear the petticoat and her, the trousers on!

(ENTER TOM THUMB)

(Aside) O ye winds above,

Now whisper dear Huncamunca's mine!

The dreadful business of war is done And beauty, heavenly beauty, crowns my toils.

I've thrown aside the bloody swords and spoils, And to pretty dances on the village green invite my bride.

(Still aside) As when some chimney-sweeper sweeps all day In

dark and dusty tunnels, at night he flies away, His hands and face to wash, and in a fresh shirt Lies down with his love to splash and splash.

C'st moi *(bows)* le plongeur!

(EXIT TOM THUMB. FARR-PARR GRIZZLE ENTERS LEFT STAGE FRONT)

KING ARTHUR: *(Aside)* Some laughter there I do declare

But here they come again, *(sniffs)* accursed similes on the air - God smite the poet who first wrote one, The devil punish every bard who uses them, Tho' I have seen some comparisons both just and true, Familiar names well known to you and I, While other wordy fools, who liken all To a block of rotten wood or cheese.

I tell you the devil's happy here, for the whole of creation, Cannot furnish an apt metaphor for his situation.

(ENTER DOLLALLOLLA. EXIT KING ARTHUR)

DOLALLOLLA: So there you are at last.

Has it come to this, then, Colonel Farr-Parr Grizzle, That you have thus come to my aid?

FARR-PARR GRIZZLE: You have something to tell me, my gracious Queen?

DOLLALLOLLA: You, a spiteful mountain of greed and treason, as ugly as Beelzebub, Must I ask you teach me to scold, instruct this bloody mouth of mine To spout out words as malicious as your own, you nasty-minded man, Words which would shame the brawling fishwives of the town.

FARR-PARR GRIZZLE: I'll say you never said a word of that, We are allies natural and courteous To the outside world, there is no conspiracy Between you and me or any Of my paid informer-patriots out there.

O please, my Queen, far from my pride it is, To think my humble tongue, your royal lips could Instruct in that art where you so excel, But may I ask, without appearing forward, Why and where you would wish to grab, and blab and stab?

DOLLALLOLLA: 'Why and where!?' By Jove, haven't you heard What every corner of the court resounds with?

That weeny Thumb will be made into a great, great man!

FARR-PARR GRIZZLE: I confess I did hear something about it,

I could easily have stopped my ears, as usual, But the grinding sounds of treachery and deceit, Set my teeth on edge and I did, perforce, listen once or twice.

DOLLALLOLLA: I would have preferred to hear at the still noon of night Warning cries of 'Rebellion!' in every street.

Hells' bells, I believe I'd hang myself like a piece of juicy meat To think I would be made a grandma by such a freak!

Oh, the King forgets that when she was with pudding, The bastard by a tinker on a stile was dropped!

O good brave Grizzle, saviour of the nation, In every bloody station, I can't bear to see this Thumb From a blancmange swell into a king, O protuberance vile, Could my sweet honeycombe Huncamunca, Ever take this filling from between the sheets?

FARR-PARR GRIZZLE: O horror, horror, horror, horror! Don't go on my Queen, Your voice like twenty screech-owls makes me cringe.

DOLLALLOLLA: Then rouse yourself, we may yet prevent this hated match.

FARR-PARR GRIZZLE: We will! And if fate itself should conspire With us to cause it, I'd swim through the seas, Ride upon the clouds, dig up the earth, blow out every fire, I'd rave, I'd rant, I'd rip, I'd roar, Fierce as the hero who overcame the singing sirens, And from poetic dangers swam to prosaic shores, I swear I'd tear the scoundrel Thumb into one and twenty pieces, Meaning 'Totals krieg!' before the peace is.

DOLLALLOLLA: Oh, yes and no! prevent the match but do not hurt him much.

For although I do not want my daughter to bend the knee, Yet can we kill the man who killed the giants?

FARR-PARR GRIZZLE: I tell you, Madame, it was all a trick.

He made the giants first, then killed them - As fox-hunters bring foxes to the wood, And set the hounds again to drink their blood.

DOLLALLOLLA: Nonsense and stuff!

Rumour and insinuation to discredit Thumb before the nation and before me!

FARR-PARR GRIZZLE: How's that?

DOLLALLOLLA: Haven't you seen the giants?

Aren't they now in the yard below, ten thousand proper ones?

FARR-PARR GRIZZLE: Indeed I can't positively tell but I firmly Believe there is not a single real one.

DOLLALLOLLA: What!? Get out of my sight, you traitor, bugger off!

By all the stars, I swear you are jealous of Tom Thumb.

Go, now go! you sniffing, shitty dog, Go cock your leg against some... nettles...or something!

FARR-PARR GRIZZLE: Madame, don't worry, I'm withdrawing now, I have removed every fiery sting from him. But I promise, Tom Thumb will feel the anger he has roused, Like two dogs fighting in the streets, When a third dog the two dogs meet, With savage teeth, they bite him to the bone, And this dog smarts for what the two nasty dogs have done.

I'll keep in touch, hypocrisy has pretty savage bites as well And well protected against the sharpest Hedges of all third-rate, ill-born similes, I go. I can fool anyone with *my* honey tongue!

(EXIT FARR-PARR GRIZZLE. QUEEN alone, paces)

DOLLALLOLLA: And which direction shall I move in now?

Where can I go? Blast and damn, I love Tom Thumb, but must not tell him, For what is a woman when her virginity's gone? - A coat without a lapel, a wig without its curls, A stocking with a gaping hole. I can't live without my virginity Or without Tom Thumb. Then let me weigh them In two equal scales, in this scale put my virginity, In that one, Tom Thumb. Oh, shit, Tom Thumb Is heavier than my virginity - but hang on a bit, Perhaps I may be left a widow, If this match is prevented, then Tom Thumb is mine, In that dear hope I will forget the strain.

And Farr-Parr Grizzle still wants my rapport, He'll set the Bailiffs one or two upon their camp, As even if, like some tart to Bridewell sent, to wind hemp And endure floggings by the score, I am still content - Because I know in time I'll ease my present pain And freely walk the streets, an honest, drunken royalwhore again!

(EXIT DOLLALLOLLA)

ACT 2 SCENE 1

(1ˢᵗ BAILIFF, 2ⁿᵈ BAILIFF armed, hiding in street)

1ˢᵗ BAILIFF: Come on, faithful friend, Bailiff to the end, Do your duty tonight and triple mugs of beer Will welcome you at home. Stay before me now, This is the way the bastard Doodle always goes, Such a 'friend' to Dollallolla, and even more her man, Plotting and planning like a fiend, Suspected by all third persons in the land.

2ⁿᵈ BAILIFF: Say no more, friend and fellow Bailiff, Every word inspires my soul with virtue, How I long to meet the enemy in the street And lay these honest hands upon his back, nab him, And drag the trembling wretch to the Debtor's dreary cell!

2ⁿᵈ BAILIFF: Then when I have him there, I will squeeze him dry, Oh, glorious thought. By the sun, moon and stars I enjoy it even now, though in thought at first, But in plain sight, it will lighten up the view!

(THEY hide in the shadows)

ACT 2 SCENE 2

(PRINCESS HUNCAMUNCA'S chambers, with Chief Lady-in-Waving MUSTACHA, waving)

HUNCAMUNCA: Give me some music to ease my heart – no, enough!

O Tom, why weren't you born of royal blood?

Why wasn't colossal Caesar your very own grandpa, And you, saintly Prince of Bradford, old and new?

. O Tom Thumb, Tom Thumb!

Wherefore art thou Tom Thumb?!

(ECHO OF HUNCAMUNCA'S words off stage as GHOST imitates her)

GHOST: Wherefore art thou, huh!

HUNCAMUNCA: Come out whoever you are, I'm not afraid of you.

GHOST: You have no reason to be afraid of me. I am your friend.

(GHOST appears back stage)

GHOST: Merlin's the name, conjuror by trade, Kin to kings and Enchanters alike, And to my art, Tom owes his very being.

HUNCAMUNCA: What? How's that?

GHOST: Have you never read my epic poem, 'The Getting of Tom Thumb?'

Listen! 'His father was a ploughman plain, His mother milked the cow, And yet the way to get a son This couple knew not how, Until such time the good old man To learned Merlin went, myself, And there to me in great distress And in great secrecy showed How in his heart he wished To have child so much, in time to come To be his heir, tho' it might be No bigger than a thumb Of whom old Merlin here did foretell That his wish he would have.

And so a son of stature small, The Enchanter gave to him And so his family moved from two to three And all lived happily. But...

MUSTACHA: ...Huncamunca, you're talking to yourself again, which must be very boring for you.

HUNCAMUNCA: Farewell, sweet, delirious shade.

(GHOST vanishes)

MUSTACHA: What on earth was that?

HUNCAMUNCA: Just Tom Thumb's wrinkled guide and mentor.

MUSTACHA: From where?

HUNCAMUNCA: Carmarthen, near Camelot.

MUSTACHA: I am surprised that your Highness can give yourself a moment's uneasiness about that insignificant little fellow. He's no better than a toy-boy for a husband, if he was my man, his horn should be as long as his tibula. If you had fallen in love with a grenadier, I should not have been surprised - if you had fallen in love with *something*, but to fall in love with nothing...!?

HUNCAMUNCA: ...now shut up your stupid point of view, it's done. Listen, The gentle winds of heaven when they blow in flowery meads, Are not so soft, so sweet, as my Thummy wummy's breath, And sometimes, even so, the dove is not so gentle to its mate.

MUSTACHA: But the dove is every bit as proper for a husband, But sad to say, there's not a Beau about the court Looks so little like a man. Thumb is a perfect butterfly, A thing without substance, almost without a shadow too.

HUNCAMUNCA: This rudeness is most undesirable, shut up your lies, I said, or I shall think this railing comes from love of the tiny man. Tom Thumb is such a creature that no one can abuse unless they love him. And I can't help my passion either, if I am also in love with Colonel Farr-Parr Grizzle, our highly principled rebel leader.

MUSTACHA: Watch out! Princess, the King's coming back!

HUNCAMUNCA: Then be off with you, I have affairs of the heart to manage, Which are infinitely harder than affairs of state.

(EXIT MUSTACHA, waving. ENTER KING ARTHUR)

ACT 2 SCENE 3

KING ARTHUR: Let all but sweet Huncamunca leave the room.

My dear daughter, I've been noticing Every day more sadness in your expression.

Your eyes, like two open windows, Used to show the beauty of the room within, Now have Venetian blinds dropped over them, What's the matter, dear daughter, what is the cause of this?

Don't you have enough to eat and drink, We've given strict orders not to stint you anything.

HUNCAMUNCA: Alas, my Lord, a tender maid like me may want

What she can neither eat nor drink.

KING ARTHUR: What is that then? Tell me.

HUNCAMUNCA: Oh, spare my blushes, I mean, a husband.

KING ARTHUR: If that is all, then I have already provided one, A husband great in arms, whose bloody sword streams With the yellow blood of slaughtered giants, Whose name is even known in Matilda's wild billabongs, Whose valour, wisdom, virtue, fame make a noise Greater than the kettle-drums of one and twenty regiments.

HUNCAMUNCA: Who is my royal father talking about?

KING ARTHUR: The great Tom Thumb.

HUNCAMUNCA: Is this really possible?

KING ARTHUR: The Venetian-blinds are gone, I see instead A village dance of joys and jigs, right now, in your face, Your eyes spit joy, your cheeks glow red as beef, For desire of mighty Tom.

HUNCAMUNCA: 'Tom!' Oh, there's magic-music in that name, Enough to turn me inside out.

Yes, I'll admit Tom Thumb is the cause of all my grief, For him I've sighed, I've wept I've gnawed my sheets.

KING ARTHUR: Oh, you won't have to gnaw your tender linen no more,babee, A husband you shall have to mumble to, instead.

HUNCAMUNCA: Oh, what happy sounds.

Let no one say my virtue's done. I am overjoyed.

KING ARTHUR: I can see you really are.

Delight lights up your eyes, And the dark frowns of your brows Fizzle out like lightning in the night, And leave your soul intact, your sorrows Blasted like small-shot through a hedge.

HUNCAMUNCA: Oh, don't say 'small.'

KING ARTHUR: This loyal news will ride post on this royal tongue, Ourself will bear the glad tidings to Tom Thumb, But don't think, dear daughter, that your powerful charms Will detain the hero from his arms, His duties are as varied as his delights, Now it is his turn to kiss, then it is to fight, And then to kiss again. Like Mighty Jove When tired of excessive thunderings above, Comes down to earth and has a quiet bit, Then flies back to his trade of reigning us again.

(EXIT HUNCAMUNCA, KING ARTHUR. Street in town, ENTER TOM THUMB, DOODLE, MUSTACHA, waving back stage)

ACT 2 SCENE 4

TOM THUMB: I'm glad we met again,

My Doodle, I am sickening very strange, For tho' I love sweet Huncamunca and her honeycombes, Yet at the thought of marriage I grow pale;

For, Oh, but swear to keep it ever secret, And I'll tell you a story that will make you stare.

DOODLE: I swear by sweet Huncamunca's charms, I'll keep it under my tongue for life, Like you, triumphant Tom, I love all salaries, Especially when discretely in my pocket.

TOM THUMB: Then know, friend Doodle, my old grandma often warned me, 'beware of marriage!'

DOODLE: Sir, I blush to think a warrior great as you, Should be frightened by his dead grandma, Can an old woman's empty fears Deter the blooming hero from the virgin's arms?

Think of the joy that will your soul embrace When in her fond embraces gripped you lie, While on her panting breast dissolved in bliss, You pour out Tom Thumb, with such an endless kiss.

TOM THUMB: O, Doodle you have fired my eager soul again, Although I know your interest dwells in one moustache as well.

In spite of my Grandma, the Princess will be mine, I'll hug, I'll caress, I'll eat her up with all my love.

Whole days and nights and years shall be too short For our enjoyment; every sun shall rise Blushing to see what antics we get up to in bed.

DOODLE: O, mon general, I will pursue this plot to the utmost, too, For dear Mustacha's sake, For St George and merry England, For

Freedom, for slaves, for women, for adolescents Human rights for all of them, the twats, that's what!

TOM THUMB: Bravely said, my Doodle.

MUSTACHA: I agree with His Highness, King Arthur Number II And with my Doodle. Like anything!!

TOM THUMB: Bravely said again.

DOODLE: I am for the victorious side in every war!

KING ARTHUR: Yes, there are never too many ' bravely saids' In our heroic kingdom! Farewell, baby!

MUSTACHA: Dig ya, man.

(MUSTACHA EXITS WAVING)

ACT 2 SCENE 5

(ENTER 1ˢᵗ, 2ⁿᵈ BAILIFF, right. They spot TOM THUMB, DOODLE)

2nd BAILIFF: You are Mr Doodle? Well, stand and deliver for the law's own sake!

1ˢᵗ BAILIFF: We have here an action taken out against you and him, A neighbour put this warrant in our hands For uttering foul calumnies against the King Drink, fornication and all kinda sin, Off to Bow Street now!

TOM THUMB: What, you dogs, arrest my friend in front of my very face?

Do you really think Tom Thumb would suffer this disgrace?

But let you vain cowards threaten with an empty word, Tom Thumb will show his indignation with his sword.

(TOM THUMB kills 1ˢᵗ and 2ⁿᵈ BAILIFFS with sword thrusts)

1ˢᵗ BAILIFF: Ah, I am hit, I'm bleeding. Look.

2ⁿᵈ BAILIFF: I'm wounded as well! See me!

To the dismal shades below This Bailiff's life must also go.

DOODLE: Go then both to Lucifer, like the villains of Hades that you are!

1ˢᵗ BAILIFF: But we'll serve well the topmost Bailiffs down in hell.

TOM THUMB: Thus perish all bailiffs in the land! Forever onwards, Till all debtors at midday can walk the streets And have no fear of one Bailiff and his lousy treats!

(1ˢᵗ, 2ⁿᵈ BAILLIF die)

DOODLE: Bravo, Tom Thumb another victory on your hands!

(EXIT TOM and NOODLE)

ACT 2 SCENE 6

(HUNCAMUNCA'S chamber, with CONSPIRATOR FARR-PARR GRIZZLE, would be suitor, of HUNCAMUNCA)

FARR-PARR GRIZZLE: Oh, sweet Huncamunca, your pouting breasts, Like cymbals of gold, give everlasting beats of joy, As bright as brass they are and just as hard, Let me caress them, O Huncamunca bright!

HUNCAMUNCA: What? You dare!? Don't you know me, Princess that I am, you dare play games with me?!

FARR-PARR GRIZZLE: O Huncamunca, I know you are a royal Princess, And daughter of a King, but love does not scorn The meanest of the tribe, nor is afraid of power, Love often takes Lords and Ladies to the cells, And commands the Guard to throw away the bells.

Nothing is too high, or low where true love dwells.

HUNCAMUNCA: But if what you said was true, my love now, I am, To another due. It's quite useless to press your suit on me, I've been promised to Tom Thumb, by order of dear daddee.

FARR PARR-GRIZZLE: Can my Princess really marry such a tiddler He's fitter for your pocket than your bed.

Listen, sweet Huncamunca, shun this worthless embryo, Never be taken between the sheets by such a titch.

Oh, let me fall into your arms and never flinch, I am a man of Thor, every straining inch And while we are in pleasure both together I'll press your soul and it will breathless music make While the whole world stands approving of your mate.

HUNCAMUNCA: If you are suggesting you can remove all official promises and engagements, just like that, your manhood is not proved at all.

FARR-PARR GRIZZLE: Let tiny Tom find some attractive dwarf, some fairy miss, Where no stool is needed to rise up to her breasts, For just a simple suck. By all the stars of fame and glory, You appear to be far more fitting for a Prussian Grenadier, And look at Atlas, one single globe upon his shoulders, But two dozen would not equal Awena's wonders.

The mountains of the moon are never flat Your Milky Ways are ever close to that.

HUNCAMUNCA: I find your words so heaven sent, I'm truly moved by all your eloquence.

FARR-PARR GRIZZLE: Oh, say that again,

And let the sound echo from one pole to another;

Let earth and sky be a kind of sacred locker, With battle-doors shut, the echoes all within, just for one hour, Lest we meet life's hangman at the door And be chained in Fleet prison, a tragic blow, So I will like an arrow fly from Cupid's bow, And get a marriage licence, directly from the Commons, And tie the knot upon a stage far from that chartered chamber, As all the powers forbid a Princess should do it on her own, For that ungodly act, breaks the right of holy kings, And poisons all their sacred veins. My quick return, Shall to you prove I travel by the post-horses Of passion, steeds some twenty hands or more in height, you'll see.

But they will seem too slow for me in flight, give me Mercury, The swiftest of the gods, whose messages, like mine, are for posterity!

We will ride together in the chariot called - ' destiny'!

(FARR–PARR GRIZZLE RUSHES OFF)

ACT 2 SCENE 6

(HUNCAMUNCA paces. ENTER TOM THUMB, looking around. HUNCAMUNCA hides behind bush)

TOM THUMB: Where is my Honeycombe Princess, where is my Huncamunca fair?

Where are those eyes, those trump-cards of adoration That lighten up my waxen soul with love? Where is that face, Made by nature in the same mould as radiant Venus?

HUNCAMUNCA: Oh, what is music to the ear that's deaf?

Or venison pie, to him who's who has no taste?

(Approaches TOM THUMB)

What do these praises now mean to me? For I am tempted by another.

TOM THUMB: 'Tempted'? - a word of many meanings - in your vocabulary, changed as soon as spoken.

HUNCAMUNCA: It is all written in the book of fate.

TOM THUMB: Then I will tear up the leaf on which it's written, and if fate doesn't like that, or won't allow so large a gap in her very scary diary, I'll blot out the ink of it, at the very least.

(TOM THUMB DEPARTS. Aside, as he exits)

And the King's dead right about these interminable bloody metaphors, like man, I don't know what!

ACT 2 SCENE 7

(HUNCAMUNCA paces. ENTER QUEEN GLUMDALCA)

GLUMDALCA: I need not ask just who you are, your brandy nose declares you ….

HUNCAMUNCA: … a most noble Princess of the blood royal, have a care, and I don't need to ask who you are either, a jenny wren could spot your lardy wobbles a mile off.

GLUMDALCA: A sad tale there, don't be bitchy, dear, a giantess I was, alas, who once made and unmade queens.

HUNCAMUNCA: The man whose chief ambition is to be my Lord and Master, destroyed those mighty giants of yours.

GLUMDALCA: Your 'Lord and Master?' Do you think that a man who once wore me as a portion of the spoils, will ever wear you for a moment?

HUNCAMUNCA: Well, may your chains be light as feathers, As my royal father did for you, For if what fate tells be true, You have dropped those fetters twenty Times a night, pulled on and off like easy boots, Your under garments in the basket, soiled as soot.

GLUMDALCA: I still glory in the number twenty-one, and when I settle down, like you, Content with only one, never ye heavens, I pray, never Change this face of mine for one as red as yours, I remain at twenty-one, pale as a silent swan!

HUNCAMUNCA: *(Seizes candle, hold it over GLUMDALCA's face)* Now let me be nearer to this enormous beauty, which captivated men and grenadiers in showers. Oh, Jesus Christ, now I look, you're as ugly as the very gargoyle itself! Ugh!

GLUMDALCA: Hell, you'd give the best piss-pots in your boudoir to be half as lovely.

HUNCAMUNCA: Since you're still going on and on about that, I'll put my beauty to the test!

See, here comes Tom Thumb. *(ENTER TOM THUMB)* Tom, I am yours if you go with me right now!

GLUMDALCA: Oh, stay with me, Tom Thumb, and you alone will fill that bed where twenty giants a night were fed.

TOM THUMB: In the back alley saw a whore shag two apprentices, One had a half crown in his hand, The other held a piece of gold, The whore grabs the half crown, And leaves the larger but the baser coin!

GLUMDALCA: We don't need a monarch to interpret that!

(HUNCAMUNCA grabs TOM THUMB by the hand, they run off, laughing, EXIT)

GLUMDALCA: So I'm left scorned and rejected For such a chit of a silly virgin, am I? I feel storms Now rising in my breast, tempests and whirlwinds Shriek and roar, I am all hurricanoes! The four winds Of the world are pent up inside my carcass, where Confusion horror, murder, guts and death reside.

As you can gather, I am no lamb inside.

Let Tom just wait, I sense a bloody fate!

ACT 2 SCENE 8

(KING wanders on, distraught. Brightens when he sees GLUMDALCA)

GLUMDALCA: Come, love, lay your troubles on my bare warm shoulders.

What's the matter, my Leigey, I ask only Because I know you are in love with me.

KING ARTHUR: Sure there was never so sad a King as I.

My life's a ragged coat like a beggar's, A Prince, let alone a King Should throw that garment off, To love a captive and a tender giantess is best.

GLUMDALCA: Oh, my Love!

KING ARTHUR: What a great Queen you are, my tongue is your trumpet, And your music works inside me, unknown to other men.

Oh, Glumdalca, heaven designed you as a giantess But an angelic soul you turned out to be, help me, I am a walking multitude of family griefs and burdons of state, And only on your lips is any comfort found, I'll take nature's cure that will my ills confound If immediately you lay your garments down upon the ground.

Oh, glory be, what is this I see!

GLUMDALCA: What is this I hear?

KING ARTHUR: Oh, amorous queen.

GLUMDALCA: Oh, randy King!

(KING ARTHUR and GLUMDALCA make love. Fade to violins)

ACT 2 SCENE 9

(HUNCAMUNCA, TOM THUMB, PARSON, as at a marriage ceremony)

PARSON: Happy is the wooing, that's not long a'doing, my children, For if I guess aright, Tom Thumb this night, Will give his being yet another light.

TOM THUMB: All my efforts will be to that end, Parson.

HUNCAMUNCA: Please, Tom Thumb, you make me blush.

PARSON: It is the virgin's sign and suits her well.

TOM THUMB: I don't know where, or how, or what I am, I'm so transported I have lost myself.

HUNCAMUNCA: Look to the stars, my Tom, they're so small, That were you lost, you'd find yourself no more, Like the unhappy semstress, who lost her needle in a pin-box in the hay, She looked and looked, but found the needle gotten clean away.

PARSON: You happy two, long may you live and love and propagate Till the whole land is peopled with Tom Thumbs, Like when in Cheshire cheeses, hungry maggots breed, And another and another still succeeds By thousands and the tens of thousands they increase Till one continuous maggot fills the rotten cheese Till they are called by their true names - Chief Ministers of State.

God protect you, my children, and all who eat in you.

(EXIT HUNCAMUNCA, PARSON, TOM THUMB)

ACT 2 SCENE 10

(DOODLE, FARR-PARR GRIZZLE in conversation)

DOODLE *(Aside):* Certainly I think Nature herself Wants to loose her adamantine chains, Unfix the universe and in a rage Hurl away her axles, locks and hinges.

All things are confused, The Queen is drunk, the Princess hitched, So it s said and not by me, The whole of nature is reversed.

FARR-PARR GRIZZLE: Rumour and speculation. Doodle, have you heard Anything of my sweet Honeycombe Huncamunca?

DOODLE: I've heard a thousand sighs today, But none from that wonderful bitch of ours, Such is sweet Huncamunca, sought by all, And the King, the Queen, the entire Court in thrall.

FARR-PARR GRIZZLE: Damn your reports, you make them up, You pilferer, as you go along, are you drunk?

I do not want to hear a single word – except ' Huncamunca here!'

DOODLE: She is probably married by this time, To some Brigadier or one or two grenadiers, perhaps, Or, perchance, O curses, some general Tom Thumb nearby!

FARR-PARR GRIZZLE: Not my Huncamunca, no! Whose fuckin'side are you on anyway?

DOODLE: On your Huncamunca's sweet side! And yours.

FARR-PARR GRIZZLE: Tom Thumb's more like.

DOODLE: Or everyman's, she's strayed so far.

FARR-PARR GRIZZLE: If that is true, then the whole of womankind is doomed.

DOODLE: If that is true, then we are doomed ourselves.

FARR-PARR GRIZZLE: By Jesus Christ, here she comes herself.

I'm not going to believe a word out of that pretty mouth, Above which sits Innocence on a royal brow ingrained.

(ENTER HUNCAMUNCA, dancing)

FARR-PARR GRIZZLE: Where has my Huncamunca been?

HUNCAMUNCA: O, here and there.

FARR-PARR GRIZZLE: Where?

HUNCAMUNCA: Errands of mercy

DOODLE: For whom?

HUNCAMUNCA: Mankind.

DOODLE: Then god have mercy on us all.

FARR-PARR GRIZZLE: Never! See here, I have the marriage licence in my hand.

HUNCAMUNCA: Poor old Tom Thumb.

FARR-PARR GRIZZLE: Why are you talking about him?

HUNCAMUNCA: Poor little man.

FARR-PARR GRIZZLE: Are you leading me on?

HUNCAMUNCA: Mum, mum! and mum again.

FARR-PARR GRIZZLE: Your every stupid word is 'mum.'

HUNCAMUNCA: Tom Thumb was overcome.

FARR-PARR GRIZZLE: You force me to answer you now.

No more Tom Thumb, I'm on the wrack,

I'm in the flames! 'Tom bloody Thumb,' you love that name, So lovely is that word to you, if you were dumb, You'd somehow find a voice to shout out 'Tom Thumb!

HUNCAMUNCA: Don't be so hasty about my so-called damnation My big heart for more than one has room, Heaven formed a beauty like me For at least two more.

I married him and now I'll marry you.

FARR-PARR GRIZZLE: What! You flaunt your treacheries to my face?

You think that I could fill your husband's place Because that office needs another officer, Since you scorn to enjoy one main dish You shall not have the tainted tiddler fish, The sole duty of your husband is to your Highness, But I will bear the pain, but never unrevenged Wear the slighted willow berry in my lapel, My brooding gloomy tempests are now confined, Within the hollow caverns of my mind, But they will ever whirl along the coasts, And drown the men of many boats, And then dip down into the circle known as seven, To cram every chink of hell with hideous spectres I have seen on dark and wintery days, As sudden storms rush down the highway of the sky, Sweep through the streets' - here comes the deadly simile - And with terrible ding dongs of pots and pans, Gush through spouts to sweep whole crews along Drown crowded shops, throngs of hopping vermin, The dirty and the clean together, Even the filthy chimney sweeps are now washed.

So universal hygiene is enjoyed by all, The future and the past!

HUNCAMUNCA: *(Aside)* Oh, will the crazed Farr-Parr Grizzle,

In the rashness of his fury slay My hapless bridegroom on his wedding day?

I, who this morn, of two, chose both to wed Must go tonight alone to bed?

Yes, once I have seen a wild fool with a choice like this, Try to give preference to both, Coveting to sit on one, and the other, too, But the two stools did her confound, She found herself between them, squatting on the ground.

But Farr-Parr has a silver tongue, And has my affection sorely wrung, Shall I say 'yes' or 'no' to either, Or 'yes' and 'no' to neither?

(FARR-PARR GRIZZLE chases HUNCAMUNCA off stage. EXIT BOTH)

ACT 2 SCENE 11

(FADE ON GHOST)

GHOST: Hail, you black horrors of midnight's noon, You fairies, goblins, bats and foul owls, all hail!

> Oh, you mortal watchmen, from whose throat, The immortal phantoms dread croakings rise, You prancing apparitions who by day condemned to die In elemental pyres, now play in church yards, Skip over our graves to the loud music of a silent bell!

> All Hail! King Arthur Two, what does it mean to you?

> *(SPOT ON KING ARTHUR, drinking side stage)*

KING ARTHUR: Where is my Glumdalca now? I love her truly, Every inch was bliss. But when she rolled off me, I was flatter than a pancake really.

GHOST *(OFF STAGE):* Too whit, twohoo!

KING ARTHUR: What bloody noise is that? What swine dares At this time of night, profane the peace with cacophony Of voice and feet?

(GHOST comes forward)

GHOST: One who defies your empty power to hurt him, One who dares to walk into your bed chamber, unannounced.

KING ARTHUR: You presumptuous slave, you penurious yob, You vacant lot, I'll have you put to the stake.

GHOST: Frighten other people with that up 'em OK, But I am a ghost and am already dead, Over and done with as a man of flesh and genius.

> Bloody heavens above, you stars –

It is better that your last hour had come For that hour is now extended by at least a tun, Fifty by fifty times a slow death and all for fun!

Don't worry, I'll drag you forward by your shroud, Every second squeeze you like a bladder So you can piss your life away, Because you do not really matter. Goodnight!

(MAKES TO LEAVE)

KING ARTHUR: So you're running away, is it? Just as well I was wondering just what courage a ghost might have.

And you can't say I said that, since you have no breath to speak of.

Don't dare walk into my chambers once again, On pain of being cast away on the sands, As sure as guns go 'bang, bang! Bang!'

I'll have you on the wrack prepared to hang, I'll fill that Red Sea full of loathsome gin The stink alone kills cats from twenty paces, Ruins mothers and their kin, I'd dunk you in, I promise, you, the last sodden sample of the lowest races.

GHOST: Ha, says you! Ha, says I, for King Arthur II, Whose father's ghost I know as well as Thumb's, Two for the price of one, back in the day well known As mighty Arthur Number One. Now I see, It's true, even those who drive a coach and horses Soon make forgotten corpses.

KING ARTHUR: Not for Arthur Two, for Number one was number two's true father.

I see you now, you really are the honest pere of Number Two, And I am me twice over and so is Tom. I thought you were kidding first.

GHOST: Here I am, an authentic infinite shade!

KING ARTHUR: Then let me press you in my arms You spirit multiple, you best of ghosts, You're something more than insubstantial now!

GHOST: I wish I was something more as well So we could feel each other in a warm embrace.

But now I have the advantage over you, For while I feel you, you can't feel me.

KING ARTHUR: But tell me, you fine piece of fancy atmosphere, tell me What terribly important business brings You back down here to the baleful earth?

GHOST: Ok, then, be ready, be advised, The land is full of slaughters, Enough to send you packing home.

Listen, *(Sound of mob off stage)* hear that?

Your subjects, en masse, are perfectly revolting, Up in arms, led by the forked-tongue Grizzle.

KING ARTHUR: I suspected all along, you know, I shall have him shovelled into dung Like a beetle on its back, the bum!

GHOST: I observed it too, when rosy-fingered dawn arose To open the revealing shutters of the sky, It exposed your royal palace quite a lot, So I have seen bees in clusters forming up, I have seen regiments of stars on frosty nights, I have seen the sands of time on windy days, I have seen the shades on Pluto's ghastly shores, I have seen daisies dance in Spring, I have seen the leaves of Autumn fall, I have seen the apples of summer smile on me, I have seen the snows of Winter's icy frowns, I have seen...

KING ARTHUR: ...Oh, fuck what you have seen!

Have you come down here as Arthur's phantom next of kin

To abuse me with endless similes To keep me on a verbal wrack.

Bugger off, my mind is full of triple meanings now, All made worse by two-faced traitors, I have grizzles to erase, not make.

Go! Or by all the torments of married bliss, I'll run You through the body although you have none!

GHOST: Watch it, O King, the woods are on the move, I will leave you now, not frightened By your voice or temper, Bless you my son's son's son, And my son's remembrancer, myself, And Merlin too Cherchez la fame, I suppose, But you're right, where is sweet Huncamunca Honeycombe...?

KING ARTHUR: ...leave her out of this!

GHOST: Be warned by cockerels such as chanticleer.

I will warn you formally now come what may, King Arthur Two! Beware! Beware! Beware!

And try to avoid your impending fate For if you are killed today Tomorrow all your care will come too late.

KING ARTHUR: Hang on a minute, sprite chappy, misty kin, Don't leave me in this uncertain state, So when you tell me what my fate is, Teach me how to avoid it.

(ASIDE, to audience) A moment alone with you lot.

All of you, join in the universal condemnation Of 'like' and 'as', as very sick figures of speech.

Curst be the poet who first ever wrote a bloody simile!

Damn every bard who used them publically, tho' I have seen Some whose comparisons are both just and true, While other wordy fools liken all To a block of rotten wood or Cheshire cheese.

I tell you, Lucifer is happy here, for the whole of creation
Cannot furnish apt metaphors for his wicked situation.

Thanks for listening. Back to the fray.

Now what to do about one Colonel Farr-Parr Grizzle and the
nation?

GHOST *(Shouting off stage):* Good luck, tough shit, my son! Think on it!

KING ARTHUR: I'll give it my most serious consideration, sir.

ACT 2 SCENE 12

(ENTER QUEEN DOLALLOLLA, steals up to KING)

DOLLALLOLLA: Why, my heart's King Arthur Number II,

Do you sneak away from these my breasts?

Why do you leave me alone in the dark When you know I'm scared of ghosts And dogs in the night that bark?

KING ARTHUR: Oh, Dollallolla, blame love, my love, I'd hoped the fumes of last night's Punch had shut your eyes tight as a stone.

(ASIDE) A moment again. But I have found that there's no potency In wee drams for tender horny wives, Who wake and ride upon their husbands After two quarts of gin or more, But what even bigger surprise awaits For wives to wake up with the sun, To find their Romeos vanished, Then reaching out with grasping arms Finds her deserted for a limp and useless bolster In spite of her ever willing charms.

Reflect well on that, my Queen, I have read all about it in Ovid's Metamorphosis, How Jove in an inanimate form Lay with lovely Diana, trust me in my myths, Sometimes I thought the bolster was my Diana, Or something like that, I think.

Now come back to me, you most virtuous of your sex, Oh, Dollallolla, if only wives were all like you, Husbands in their beds would sprout no horns, Or ladies hide them in a better place;

If sweet Huncamunca inherits just a part of you, Tom Thumb indeed is blessed in bed and board, Tom Thumb! Oh, that fatal name, If only you knew what I knew, you'd know-

-yes, just what you'd know, like a starfish in the sand.

DOLLALLOLLA *(Aside)*: Such sticky pastry metaphors, Where does he find them? I can't make out one word.

Tell me, Arthur, why do you always announce, like those men Who travel freak shows about the countryside, With 'now you will see what you will see,' why?

So, come on, tell me more, now you have told me quite enough.

(ENTER DOODLE in a rush)

DOODLE: Great Arthur Two and sloshed Dollallolla One!

May you both be blessed with ever such long lives, I beg you now, hear a most dolorous dirge, News these two bickering physicians bear.

(EXIT NOODLE. ENTER 1st, 2nd PHYSICIANS, Dr C HURCHYARD and Dr FILLGRAVE, bickering)

FILLGRAVE: We attend your Majesty's command, however, lugubrious, From the fields of ignominious defeat.

KING ARTHUR: 'Defeat?' Never! 'Ignominious'? perhaps…

DR CHURCHYARD: The great Tom Thumb is gone, gone, In spite of my most prime medicaments.

DR FILLGRAVE: Mine too.

DOLLALLOLLA: Gone!? Woe, woe and woe again!

KING ARTHUR: This is passing sudden. To what distemper did the great Tom Thumb succumb?

DR CHURCHYARD: He died, may it please your majesty, of a distemper called Diarmorphine, Spotted by the second Chief Surgeon's sixth assistant, Dr AP Galen, of Rome. When the great Tom had, in the heat of battle, sudden bouts of giddiness, I bled him, then applied mustard poultices, glister for blisters, the devil's claw for gripes, then a purge, a vomit, then came the stools and all that crap Diarmorphine was the name of the game.

DR FILLGRAVE: No, it was not. I tell you, you're making a big mistake, it was not Diamorphine,it was Peripilisis! If he'd broken his arm, I would have cut it off, if he'd had a headache, I would have peeled off his scalp, then and only then, I would have given my special Emetics and Diaretics. Your Majesties, I assure you the symptoms of Peripilisis, are very various, varied, uncertain and doubtful, but I know them like the back of my hand. Dead as a doornail. Sorry.

(TOM THUMB rushes on flourishing a bloody sword)

TOM THUMB: Your Majesties, Arthur Two, Dollallolla One, a great victory has blessed our arms.

DOCTORS FILLGRAVE, CHURCHYARD: Jesus Christ, not him!

KING ARTHUR: You still live!?

DOLLALOLLA: You blazing stars above, can this be true, or is it an Illusion I see before my eyes?

KING ARTHUR: And you have not been dead at all?

TOM THUMB: Not one itsy, bitsy little bit!

DOLLALLOLLA: Thank God you have not changed.

TOM THUMB: Hear you! Farr-Parr Grizzle with a bold rebellious mob, Advanced upon the Palace, threatening every gate, But the Princess sweet Huncamunca, I delivered straight, Triumphant as the Tom who stands before you now, Without my iron helmet in place maybe, But I will soon, too, set the people free Guided by divine right and royal Liberty!

But where is my sweet, sweet Huncamunca?

There was a rumour among the Grenadiers, She was mistaken for a bride. She stood outside The fray a moment or two, a bravura bravado!

Then sped the bloody field like a lamb from slaughter Give her my eternal love, however faint the laughter.

DR FILLGRAVE: Hey, what about us?

TOM THUMB: There you still are, you carvers of the dead! Bugger off!

DR GRAVEYARD: We've come all this way...

DR FILLGRAVE: ...and it was costly too.

DR GRAVEYARD: I told you it was Peripilisis...

DR FILLGRVE: ...it was Diamorphine!

KING ARTHUR: Get outta in here!

DR FILLGRAVE: We've lost our reputation, Mr Graveyard, and what is worse, our double fee, I fear.

DR GRAVEYARD: Damn all monarchs, the trick did not work this time, Mr Fillgrave

DR FILLGRAVE: It will next time, Dr Graveyard, there are plenty left.

(EXIT 1st, 2nd PHYSICIAN, Doctors FILLGRAVE and GRAVEYARD)

TOM THUMB: False physicians to a man, Chief Poisoners

To the State, part of the conspiracy to throw The people down the drains, with broken hearts and gins, And cast aspersions on my longevity, Foul Grizzle, footling rebels, all drowning in their piddle.

I go now, and it won't be long before I return, Being the protagonist in practically every scene, Wait for me, in joyousness, of course, but in patriotism also, Sweet Huncamunca will answer all your questions in a moment.

ACT 2 SCENE 13

(EXIT TOM THUMB, flourishing sword, meets PRINCESS HUNCAMUNCA, they embrace, EXIT, sound of love making)

VOICE of **KING ARTHUR**: Good lad! Go to it!

VOICE of **DOLLALLOLLA**: Brave lass! Go to it!

(Sound of love making, with sound of battle. PAUSE. ENTER PRINCESS HUNCAMUNCA, tidying herself. ENTER DOLLALLOLLA, KING)

KING: You look exhausted, my daughter, but satisfied, like humanity at its peak.

DOLLALLOLLA: I know where in the hell you've been and so does your Dad here, so belt up. But where has Tom Thumb gone?

HUNCAMUNCA: Well, I 'm not sure for now, but half a minute ago

He sallied out to encounter the two-faced foe, Piddle and Co, and swore, if fate has not deserted him, From his shoulders he'd cut vile Grizzle's head And serve him up as chocolate in your bed!

KING ARTHUR: Such down-to-earth loyalty! Come Ladies, Stay with me, as one, we'll wait for Tom Thumb's victory.

DOLLALLOLLA: Tho' giants conspire with Grizzle and the gods, Tom Thumb alone is equal to all the sods!

He is indeed a breastplate to us all!

While he fights for us, we need not fear at all, His martial arm performs our very wish And serves up every foe in many a gravy dish.

KING ARTHUR: Let the mistress of this house have pause

While the cook presents the bill of fare, Whether cod, that northern king of fish, Or duck, or goose, or pig adorn our forks

However many guests appear, regardless of their sex and number, She sets their dinners now without a single blunder.

Let's go now, and celebrate the decanting of many tops of bottles.

DOLLALLOLLA: You are so insightful, I have the thirst of a Dutchman's dredger.

(EXIT GLUMDALCA, KING ARTHUR, HUNCAMUNCA)

ACT 2 SCENE 14

(TOM THUMB wonders on and off looking upwards)

TOM THUMB: I have never seen such a day as this!

How the weather change with our fortunes, The still born thunder rumbles overhead As the gods unhinge the world, And heaven and earth in confusion hurl Their darts upon the earth.

Yet will I tread upon thus tottering ball Until Farr-Parr has his inevitable fall.

(EXIT TOM THUMB. ENTER PARR-FARR GRIZZLE, DOODLE)

FARR-PARR GRIZZLE: So far our arms with victory are crowned, Tho' we have fought one or two or three or four, Yet we have found no further enemy to draw.

DOODLE: But I would cheerfully avoid today To engage our foes, for it is the first of April, as it goes.

FARR-PARR GRIZZLE: Today of all days I'd choose, For on this day my dear Mum was born, You watch, I'll make Tom Thumb into such a Fool.

I'll send his wits on errands he's never heard of, To weep among the flames of hell below.

DOODLE: I'm happy to find our armies are so stout, By god, they knock the opposition out, Nor does it move my wonder less to know How we came to be so strong, Let's talk about it as we march along, There are two sides to every confrontat-i-o-n, Especially mine, the man of common sense, Partisan of every bleeding fact-i-o-n.

(EXEUNT FARR-PARR GRIZZLE, DOODLE. ENTER TOM THUMB side stage. Shadows of TOM fighting upstage, with battle noises)

ACT 2 SCENE 15

TOM THUMB *(Aside)*: Jesus Christ, my senses are lost in amazement.

Hey, Huncamunca, Glumdanca, come on, come on!

(ENTER GLUMDANCA, HUNCAMUNCA)

Look at your Tom! yet another me. Look!

The ghost of Merlin recalls me at my best!

GLUMDALCA: Ah! No, I do not wish to look on this, A sight of horror, see, hold back, oh no!

My darling Tom, you are torn to pieces and devoured by The expanded jaws of a huge red cow!

(GHOST APPEARS SIDE STAGE)

GHOST: Don't let these sights put off your brainy mind, Tom Thumb, For, see, a sight more glorious hits your eyes, See, from afar, a theatre rises up, There are ages still unborn, And they will pay tribute To the heroic actions of today Then this burlesque tragedy At length shall choose your name As the greatest Laureate of the Game Henry bloody Fielding at his worst and best again, That's the real name of the game!

TOM THUMB: Enough, let no more war-like music sound, We fall contented if we fall renowned!

ACT 2 SCENE 16

(ENTER FARR-PARR GRIZZLE, DOODLE, with rebels. GLUMDALCA, with TOM THUMB - the two groups confront each other)

DOODLE: At last the enemy advances here and stops!

FARR-PARR GRIZZLE: I hear them with my ear, I see them with my eye. Draw your broad swords, now, curs.

DOODLE: Farr-Parr fights for liberty!

FARR-PARR GRIZZLE: - the very mustard of life!

DOODLE: I battle for both sides of the sandwich!

TOM THUMB: Are you the famous man whom famous men call 'Colonel Farr-Parr Grizzle'?

FARR-PARR GRIZZLE: Are you the much more famous man very famous men call 'Tom Thumb?'

TOM THUMB: The same.

FARR-PARR GRIZZLE: Come on, upon our bodies we will prove our worth. For free Liberty!

TOM THUMB: For free love! Charge!

DOODLE: For everyone everywhere! Charge!

(A general melee, DOODLE stands aside, FARR-PARR GRIZZLE, GLUMDALCA and TOM THUMB pause)

GLUMDALCA: Turn, you coward, you wouldn't fly from a mere giantess, would you?

FARR-PARR GRIZZLE: You're too coarse, too full of cellulite to fight.

GLUMDALCA: Stop this my thrust to your heart then.

FARR-PARR GRIZZLE: No, I'm thrusting at yours.

GLUMDALCA: Fuck, you've pushed too hard, you've run me through the guts.

FARR-PARR GRIZZLE: Then that's the end of one at least.

GLUMDALCA: No, it's not, I'm tough as shit, and still got lines to speak.

TOM THUMB: And when you're dead, Farr-Parr Grizzle, boy, that's the end of two, Both rebels to the cause – the cause – myself, not you!

FARR-PARR GRIZZLE: Don't you come all triumphal over me!

DOODLE: Under all the bombast I was true to King Arthur II of the Brythons.

See how I'm standing at your side, Ready to repel any creeping marine commandoes inside!

FARR-PARR GRIZZLE: Sweet Honeycombe Huncamunca is still mine!

TOM THUMB: Take that! *(Stabs him, GRIZZLE falls)*

FARR-PARR GRIZZLE: You won't enjoy the Princess undisturbed, I'll send my ghost to fetch her to the other world As mere bait for heaven, then she shall return.

But Oh! I feel death rumbling in my brains, Some kinder sprite knocks softly on my soul, And gently whispers me to haste away;

I come, I come, most willingly I come, As when some city wife longs for country air To Hampstead or Highgate does repair, Her husband in a hurry implores her at the door And cries, 'my dear, the coach is at the door.'

With equal wish, desirous to be gone, She gets into the coach and shouts 'Drive on!'

And so do I! Aaaah! *(DIES)*

TOM THUMB: With these last words he vomits up his soul, Which, like whipped cream, the devil swallows whole.

Bear off the body now and cut off the head, Which I will to the king in triumph lug;

The rebellion's dead, their goose is cooked And now my breakfast is prepared.

(DOODLE salutes TOM. TOM THUMB, GLUMDALCA, EXIT. GRIZZLE, dead on floor)

ACT 2 SCENE 17

(COURT, KING ARTHUR II, QUEEN DOLLALOLLA, GLUMDALCA, MUSTACHA waving. COURTIERS)

KING: So Grizzle is no more!

> Open the prisons, set the wretches free, Order our treasurer to disburse six pounds To pay their debts. Let no one weep today, Come, Dollallolla... – aside - curse that stupid name, It is so long it takes an hour to speak.

> By heavens, I'll change it to 'Fido' Or some other civil monosyllable That will not tire my tongue, And ' Glamulca's just as bad.

> Come, dear, sit you down, And from my throne right here, Let's watch the courtiers bow in fear.

> Tell them to come forward.

> This is the wedding day of our dear Princess and brave Tom Thumb, Tom Thumb, who wins two victories today, And this way marches back, bearing Grizzle's head...

(DOODLE dashes on, in a sweat)

DOODLE: Oh monstrous, terrible, dreadful, heinous!

> Deaf are my ears to it, and my eyes blind, Dumb my tongue, feet lame! all senses lost!

> Howl wolves, grunt bears, hiss snakes, shriek, you ghosts...

KING: ...what is this blockhead talking about?

DOODLE: I mean, my Leige, only to lace this tale with a little decent horror.

> Well here goes - while I was in my garret two stories high, I was no turncoat ever, I looked down into the streets below And saw Tom Thumb surrounded by a mob - Two hundred apprentices

out for blood, twenty-one shoe-boys, Hackney coachmen in a line behind the whores, Assorted chimney sweeps, fish wives, swearing at themselves, And born on high, aloft, the very bloody head of Farr-Parr himself.

When, all of sudden through the streets there came A big red cow, of larger than usual size, And in a moment... or guess, You can guess the rest, Tore up Tom Thumb like a rat Between a terrier's paws, And before you could say, Oh, No, Swallowed the pieces whole!

The dead body of Tom Thumb is now no more.

GLUMDALCA: Woe, woe, I was dead right, spot on, sad too say!

KING ARTHUR: Let it be, let it be, this night has cured Your love for me, and mine for you, no doubt of it . Dollallolla is my only hope.

Lock up all the lock-ups all over again, Order my Treasurer not to give out a single farthing.

Hang all the culprits, guilty or not, it doesn't matter.

Ravish the virgins in the streets, Schoolmasters whip the boys, and more.

Let bankers, lawyers and estate agents loose To cheat and rob and ruin the world, Bury the babes as they poke their noses out Of their bloodied wombs Of this crook'd and silly universe...

...Christ, I think her Majesty's going to faint...

DOODLE: Not yet, gracious Dolallolla, peerless Queen, I have no more news.

ACT 2 SCENE 18

(GHOST OF TOM THUMB APPEARS)

GHOST: Yes, Tom Thumb, I am here again, but hardly alive,

My body is in the cow but my spirit in here thrives.

(GHOST OF FARR-PARR GRIZZLE appears)

FARR-PARR GRIZZLE: Mine too. O you stars, my vengeance is restored,

You'll never get past me now, for I will kill your ghost!

(GRIZZLE KILLS TOM THUMB'S GHOST)

GLUMDALCA: Barbarous felon! You've gone and killed the best ghost in the land.

HUNCAMUNCA: I shall still dream of him in my bed!

GLUMDALCA: No you shan't! Take that! *(Kills HUNCAMUNCA)* And that! *(Kills FARR-PARR GRIZZLE)*

DOODLE: You great big fat murderess! Take that!

(KILLS GLUMDALCA)

DOLLALLOLLA: My champion gone! And with my own fruit knife! Take that!

MUSTACHA: Save me, my Doodle!

DOODLE: Save me, my Mustacha!

KING ARTHUR: I knew Doodle for the filthy double agent he always was! And your waving was always third rate! Come on missus, stand by your man!

(DOLLALLOLLA, and KING kill DOODLE, MUSTACHA)

DOODLE *(Dying)*: Take that! The end of kings!

KING ARTHUR: End you too! Take that!

DOLLALLOLLA: For all your fucking around!

(Stabs KING. KING ARTHUR, dying, turns knife on himself, to himself)

Only myself can do royalty like me!

(Stabs himself)

As when the child whom Nurse from mischief guards, Sends Jack the Bastard with a pack of cards Kings, queens, knaves and all are at instant risk And mow each other down, Till the whole lot of them Lie scattered and overthrown, *(To AUDIENCE)* So are all our packs upon the floor are cast, All I can boast is that I fell the last!

(KING ARTHUR DIES. CUT LIGHTS. CAST LINE UP FOR CURTAIN CALL. ENTER SIR ROBERT WALPOLE, in a rage, flourishing cane)

SIR ROBERT: Stay where you are! *(Shouts to off stage)* Secretary, call the Constable and take all this down! Which one of you said it, yes, that even I 'had my price?' do I? And our royals live in 'sties?' Who said that? You*! (ACTOR falls on knees. SIR ROBERT Thrashes him. ACTOR whispers)* O, it was an ad lib, you say, can't remember. You mock *me*, you mock my office of Prime Minister, you mock the king, you mock the kingdom! The last straw! Too many plays, too many libels. Never again! I'll soon see you out of work, not only will I now strictly control you vagabonds through my Office of the King's Revels, and my licenses to perform plays, you can now add texts to that, the scripts submitted to my department before any license is even considered. The stage will be cleansed of these criminal slanders, especially against me! *(Listens)* Where? Yes, well, the Lord Chamberlain's Office will do. Who's in place there now? *(Listens)* Yes, oh, yes, Odell, didn't he write a poem or two in praise of my Bills and Acts. Yes, he'll do too. He can be my first official departmental Reader of Plays. Yes, close this Hay theatre forthwith, ban that burlesque and put this Fielding out to fallow. And so great is my influence, I will see that this censorship lasts until 1968, such is the misplaced toleration of our people. Why, you ask - because I said so. Don't any of you decent folk worry, I have legions of patriotic spies to watch over you, down to your very naked thoughts, pounds, shillings and pence. Off with the play! And so to bed, *(winks)* if you see what I mean! *(CUT LIGHTS. EXIT SIR ROBERT WALPOLE SHOUTING)* Secretary, call my constables! *(YELLS)* Curtain! (To AUDIENCE, nastily) And I mean it.

CURTAIN

Lightning Source UK Ltd.
Milton Keynes UK
UKOW06f0917041115

262058UK00002B/81/P